Choosing a Community Service Career

Other titles in the series Life—A How-to Guide

Dealing With Stress
A How-to Guide
Library ed. 978-0-7660-3439-6
Paperback 978-1-59845-309-6

Friendship
A How-to Guide
Library ed. 978-0-7660-3442-6
Paperback 978-1-59845-315-7

Getting Ready to Drive
A How-to Guide
Library ed. 978-0-7660-3443-3
Paperback 978-1-59845-314-0

Getting the Hang of Fashion and Dress Codes
A How-to Guide
Library ed. 978-0-7660-3444-0
Paperback 978-1-59845-313-3

Using Technology
A How-to Guide
Library ed. 978-0-7660-3441-9
Paperback 978-1-59845-311-9

Volunteering
A How-to Guide
Library ed. 978-0-7660-3440-2
Paperback 978-1-59845-310-2

Choosing a Community Service Career

Life
A
How-to
Guide

A
How-to
Guide

Amy Graham

Enslow Publishers, Inc.
40 Industrial Road
Box 398
Berkeley Heights, NJ 07922
USA

http://www.enslow.com

Library of Congress Cataloging-in-Publication Data
Graham, Amy.
Choosing a community service career : a how-to guide / Amy Graham.
p. cm. — (Life: a how-to guide)
Includes bibliographical references and index.
Summary: "Readers will learn about a variety of different careers in the community service field including police officers, emts, firefighters, social workers, teachers, ministers, librarians, childcare workers, postal workers, and funeral directors"—Provided by publisher.
ISBN 978-1-59845-147-4
1. Social workers—Juvenile literature. 2. Social service—Juvenile literature. I. Title.
HV40.35.G73 2011
361.0023—dc22
2010024978

Paperback ISBN: 978-1-59845-312-6

Printed in the United States of America

062011 Lake Book Manufacturing, Inc., Melrose Park, IL

10 9 8 7 6 5 4 3 2 1

To Our Readers: We have done our best to make sure all Internet addresses in this book were active and appropriate when we went to press. However, the author and the publisher have no control over and assume no liability for the material available on those Internet sites or on other Web sites they may link to. Any comments or suggestions can be sent by e-mail to comments@enslow.com or to the address on the back cover.

♻ Enslow Publishers, Inc., is committed to printing our books on recycled paper. The paper in every book contains 10% to 30% post-consumer waste (PCW). The cover board on the outside of each book contains 100% PCW. Our goal is to do our part to help young people and the environment too!

Illustration Credits: All clipart © 2011 Clipart.com, a division of Getty Images. All rights reserved.; AP Images/Benjie Sanders, p. 69; AP Images/Jack Dempsey, p. 102; AP Images/Kyle Carter, p. 109; AP Images/Peter Cosgrove, p. 71; Holloman AFB/U.S. Air Force, p. 98; © jo unruh/iStockphoto.com, p. 86; © 2011 Photos.com, a division of Getty Images. All rights reserved., pp. 4, 14, 18, 20, 27, 30, 59, 77, 88; Shutterstock.com, pp. 1, 3, 6, 10, 25, 35, 37, 40, 46, 48, 51, 55, 62, 67, 80, 82, 93, 107, 112; United States Postal Service (USPS), p. 96.

Cover Illustration: Shutterstock.com (male and female firefighters).

Contents

Firefighters respond to a fire at an apartment. They put their own lives on the line every day to keep people safe.

Emergency 9-1-1

In the middle of the night, a man wakes to the insistent beeping of a smoke detector. In an instant, he is wide awake with his heart thumping wildly. He nudges his wife to wake her and then stumbles through the dark to the bedroom door. The door feels cool against his hand, and he opens it cautiously. A rush of acrid smoke enters the room, and they both begin to cough. Their young son is asleep in the room across the hall. The mother rushes in and scoops the sleeping boy up in her arms. The air in the hall is thick with smoke, but the father finds that the path to the front door is free of flames. He guides his wife and child through the smoke to safety.

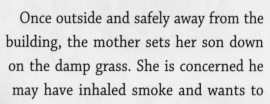

Once outside and safely away from the building, the mother sets her son down on the damp grass. She is concerned he may have inhaled smoke and wants to be certain he is conscious. The boy wakes up to his mother's worried face peering down at him. With his mind at rest that their son is safe, the father scans the house looking for the source of the smoke. With a sinking feeling, he spots bright orange flames shooting out from the windows of their attached garage. A neighbor has heard the commotion and comes across the lawn to let them know she has just called 9-1-1. The dispatcher has assured her that help is on the way. The family stands together, watching helplessly as the flames spread through their home.

Help Is on the Way

Most people are in their beds fast asleep at this time of night, but not everyone. The fire station, ablaze with lights, is a blur of activity. Firefighters, ready to go at a moment's notice, are already dressed in their protective gear. They climb aboard the fire trucks, and within seconds the trucks are pulling out onto the street with their lights flashing. As they approach an intersection, the sirens' wails cut through the quiet of the night.

Choosing a Community Service Career

A police cruiser is the first rescue vehicle to arrive at the scene. The officer was patrolling the streets in her cruiser when she heard the dispatcher's call come over the radio. Her first concern is for people's safety. She speaks with the parents: is everyone out of the burning building? The father assures the officer that no one is left inside. She turns her attention to the boy, who is coughing. She explains that an ambulance is on its way. Even as she speaks the words, the ambulance appears from around the corner. An emergency medical technician (EMT) jumps down and introduces himself to the family. He listens to the boy's breathing with a stethoscope. His partner wraps a blanket around the boy's shoulders to keep him warm.

The police officer asks if the family has any pets that may be trapped inside. They do have a cat. Could she still be in the house? They are hopeful that she has escaped out her cat door. The father enlists the neighbors' help to search the neighborhood, calling for the cat. Now the fire trucks pull up on the curb. The team of firefighters gets right to work. They listen closely to their fire chief as he scouts out the scene and shouts out orders. A firefighter drags a heavy hose from the pumper truck and attaches it to the nearby fire hydrant. They begin to spray the building with water. Other firefighters use ladders to climb onto the roof where they create vent holes to release smoke and poisonous gases created by the fire. They will put the fire out and salvage what they can of the family's property.

Emergency medical workers are quick to respond to accidents, fires, and other emergencies.

Choosing a Community Service Career

Hours later, the sun is rising over the nearby hills. The fire is out. It is clear that the garage will need to come down, but things look good for the rest of the house. The firefighters, tired and covered in soot, climb back aboard the fire trucks and return to the station. The police officer sits in her cruiser and fills out a report about the fire. The EMTs, satisfied that their work was done, returned to the dispatch center earlier. The boy is asleep on the neighbor's couch, with one arm draped over his cat. It was discovered, unhurt, hiding under a neighbor's porch. The mother and father sit together nearby, watching their son sleep. They feel sad about all they have lost in the fire. They also feel very fortunate that no one was hurt. They are very grateful to the emergency workers who have helped them.

Serving Their Communities

Public-service workers have jobs that help the people in their community. Their work is essential, whether they respond in times of emergency or help people in less dramatic ways to meet life's challenges. Teachers and child-care workers help children to learn new skills and reach their full potential. Funeral directors and social workers help people in times of great need. Librarians promote literacy and help the public to find information. Postal workers deliver letters and packages in a safe and timely manner. Police officers, firefighters, and EMTs can be counted on to be there in an emergency. Ministers give people spiritual guidance and support. Each of these fields requires people with different interests, yet all of these workers have one thing in common. They feel best about themselves when they are helping other people. These professionals are the backbone of their community. They are well respected and highly regarded community members. They take pride in what they do. Community helpers are rewarded by more than just their paychecks. They go home at the end of their day knowing that they have made a real difference in the world.

This book explores ten public-service careers. Each chapter focuses on a career. It discusses the skills and qualities that make somebody a good fit for the job. You will hear firsthand why people chose to go into their field of work and what surprised them about their jobs. You will learn about the training necessary to pursue each career path and how you can learn more if one of these careers matches your interests. Read on and find out: do you have what it takes to serve your community?

Police Officers

Chapter 2

Facts About Police Officers

- Typical duties: uphold the law, apprehend criminals, gather facts, write reports, patrol, respond to calls, serve papers, and testify in court
- Average salary: $51,410[1]
- Skills needed: leadership skills, physical strength, agility and stamina, people skills
- Basic interests: desire to work with the public, enforce law, and be a community leader
- Work environment: includes patrols, emergency situations, office work at a station or laboratory, appearances in court

When a crime is in progress, most people would run for cover. Not police officers. They are trained to confront and apprehend criminals. A police officer's job is to protect and serve. Police uphold the law. They work to keep communities safe from crime.

Most police officers work for a local police department.[2] They patrol the streets and respond to calls. They may work at the county level for the sheriff's department. Towns and cities

A police officer helps a young woman in distress.

Choosing a Community Service Career

have their own police departments. Some officers work for federal law enforcement agencies like the Federal Bureau of Investigation (FBI) or the Central Intelligence Agency (CIA). State governments also have police forces. State troopers patrol state highways. They arrest criminals who break state laws and assist local law enforcement. State game wardens specialize in hunting, fishing, and boating laws.

A Day in the Life

A police officer wears a uniform and carries a badge. During his shift, he patrols an established area. He may work alone or with a partner. Usually he drives a police vehicle such as a cruiser—a police car equipped with lights, a siren, and a police scanner. In some cases, a police officer patrols on foot, rides a bicycle or motorcycle, or even rides horseback. An officer looks for anything out of the ordinary. He must be alert and observant. He helps people who need assistance. He stops people who are breaking the law. Depending on the nature of the crime, he may let the person go with a warning. He may issue a citation (ticket) or put the person under arrest and take him or her into custody. A police officer responds to calls from a dispatcher who alerts him over the radio when

there is an accident or crime. Once on the scene, a police officer can give first aid until an EMT arrives. Police direct traffic around an accident site and try to sort out how it occurred, gathering facts and interviewing witnesses for the written report. A police officer keeps meticulous records of his actions. He writes detailed reports that are soundly based on fact. Police reports are used in court as evidence in a trial.

Some police officers undergo further training to work in special units. Some work with dogs trained to sniff out drugs or bombs. Some learn SCUBA diving and join a dive team to do underwater searches. While all police are trained in self-defense, some have extensive weapons training. They may be part of a Special Weapons and Tactics (SWAT) team. Other officers specialize in fields such as handwriting or fingerprint analysis.

Benefits and Drawbacks

Salaries vary from agency to agency. Police can retire after twenty-five years of service and draw a generous pension. A police officer usually has little problem finding a job. All communities need police officers. On the downside, a police

16

officer often works nights, weekends, and holidays. His schedule may be the opposite of his friends and family who work a typical nine-to-five day, five days a week. Police work can be dangerous. A police officer must be willing to take risks. Police work is also stressful. Police officers see the worst of human behavior. They also witness death and violence. Police need to be mature and able to handle emotional trauma.

Why Do People Become Police Officers?

Police officers feel a strong sense of responsibility. They are people who take charge. They want to make a difference in their community. Police work is a way they can serve others.

Training and Education

A police officer needs to have a high school diploma. Some agencies look for a college degree in criminal justice or police science. When a candidate applies for a job, he or she must first pass a battery of tests. There is an oral board, a physical exam, a medical exam, a polygraph test, a background check, and then a final interview. After this, the agency sends the officer to a police academy. This is an intensive training that can last anywhere from twelve to twenty or more weeks. While at the academy, students attend classes all day and into the night. They study constitutional law, civil rights, and state law.

Officers depend on a variety of elements to do their jobs, from high-tech squad cars to police dogs.

Choosing a Community Service Career

They learn how to patrol and investigate accidents. They learn about domestic violence and how to resolve conflicts. They are taught self-defense, including how to use firearms and other weapons. Students at the police academy practice first aid and emergency response.

Advancement Opportunities

For the first few months of work, a police officer is on probation. A new police officer works with a field-training officer. The field-training officer judges whether the police officer is a good fit for the job. Only after the probation is over can the officer

What Skills and Qualities Must a Police Officer Have?

- Quick to act
- Brave
- Honest
- Responsible
- Sound judgment
- Remains calm under stress
- Emotionally mature
- Physically fit
- Willing to work in dangerous conditions
- Observant
- Able to multitask

A police officer takes a report from a citizen. Accurate record keeping is a crucial part of good police work.

Choosing a Community Service Career

apply for a promotion. A police officer can advance in two ways. The first is to become a detective. A detective works to solve unresolved crimes. She wears plain clothes rather than a uniform. She gathers evidence. She interviews people. In urban areas, a detective may specialize in one area of crime. She may focus on drug trafficking or on homicide cases. A police officer can also advance in rank by becoming a field supervisor. Someone with proven leadership skills can continue to advance from corporal to sergeant, lieutenant to captain, to the top job of chief of police.

Surprising Fact

Police officers fill out a lot of paperwork. Every call for service requires them to write a report.

Job Growth and Salary Outlook

Jobs in this field will grow at an average pace. There are usually plenty of jobs for police in local police forces. Higher paying jobs at the state and federal levels are harder to get. The strongest applicants have college or military police experience.[3] The average salary for a local police officer was $51,020 in 2008. A state trooper averaged $57,270. A federal officer's annual earnings were $46,620.[4] Total earnings are often more than these salaries because of additional pay for overtime. Officers are expected to work many hours of overtime.

How Can I Learn More?

Contact your local police department. Ask if they offer a pre-law enforcement training program. If you want to do police work, do your best in school. Good reading, writing, and public speaking skills are all useful tools to have. Participate in sports to stay in shape and build your teamwork skills. Keep out of trouble. All police officers undergo background checks.

Is This Career for You?

In thinking about becoming a police officer, consider the following questions:

- Are you good at talking with people?

- Does it appeal to you to protect people in danger?

- Do you keep a level head in an emergency?

- Is physical fitness an important part of your lifestyle?

- Would your teachers, parents, and friends describe you as responsible and trustworthy?

- Are you good at thinking on your feet?

- Do you have a commanding presence?

EMTs

Chapter 3

Facts About EMTs

- Typical duties: first to respond at scene of accidents and emergencies, assess and stabilize patients, transport patients to medical facilities
- Average annual salary: $33,020[1]
- Skills needed: physical strength, quick reaction time, ability to work as part of a team, levelheadedness in emergency situations
- Basic interests: must like working in fast-paced, high-stakes situations
- Work environment: all types of weather and settings
- Schedule: often long, irregular hours

An emergency medical technician (EMT) is often the first to respond at the scene of an emergency. An EMT works as part of a team of medical professionals. An EMT's job is to help people who are sick or injured. An EMT stabilizes patients and then transports them to a hospital where they can get further treatment. An EMT must act quickly and confidently.

A Day in the Life

An EMT may work for a hospital or a private ambulance service. Police and fire departments hire EMTs, too. On a typical day, an EMT waits to be dispatched to the scene of a medical emergency. While he waits, he and his coworkers check over their ambulance. He makes sure the vehicle is clean and well stocked with supplies. He checks the ambulance itself to be sure it is in good working order. His team must be ready to go at a moment's notice.

When they get the call, they waste no time in getting to the scene. Ambulances respond to car accidents and crime scenes. They also help people who are experiencing heart attacks, strokes, or breathing difficulties. Occasionally they help pregnant women who have gone into labor. An EMT's first task is to assess the patient's condition. He tries to determine whether the patient has any preexisting medical issues. An EMT works under the supervision of a trained physician. He carefully follows the doctor's written instructions, or protocol, on how to handle different medical situations. One EMT drives the ambulance while another cares for the patient during the drive to the emergency room (ER). Some EMTs transport patients on board a helicopter. During the trip to the emergency room, an EMT monitors the patient's vital signs. Upon arrival at the ER, the EMTs transfer the patient to the medical facility staff. An EMT explains the situation and describes the actions he has taken to help the patient.

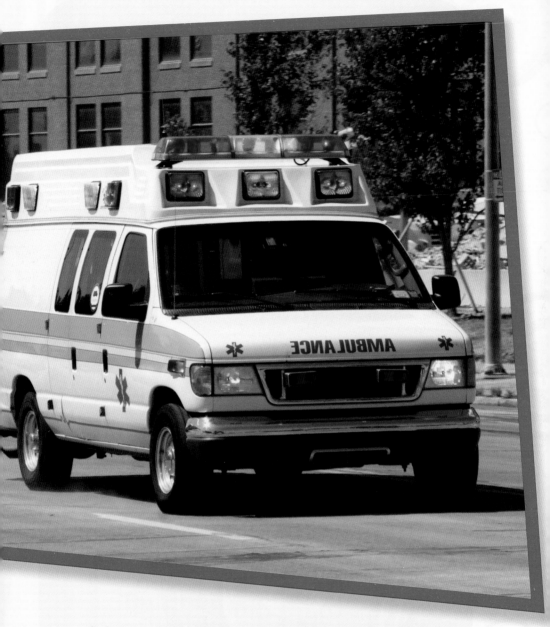

An ambulance rushes to the scene of an accident. For EMTs, each shift brings situations that require quick thinking and decisive action.

Once the EMT and his team have transferred their patient, they clean and restock the ambulance. They must be prepared for the next emergency. EMTs also transport patients from one medical facility to another.

Benefits and Drawbacks

EMTs are drawn to the excitement and challenge of the work. Every shift is sure to bring a situation that requires quick thinking and fast action. They thrive in fast-paced situations where every second counts. EMTs feel fulfilled knowing that the work they do is a vital service. Those who work as part of a police or fire department often have excellent benefits. For example, they may retire after twenty to twenty-five years of service. Then they continue to receive half their pay after they retire.[2] However, the job is a tough one. EMTs work outside in all types of weather. They kneel, squat, and carry heavy loads every time they work. Over time, these physical demands can take a toll.

Choosing a Community Service Career

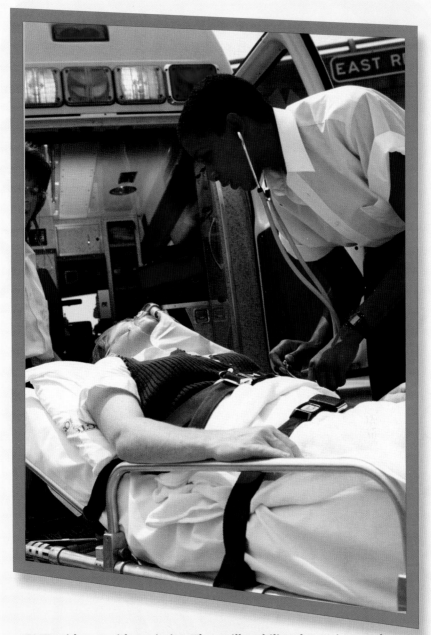

EMTs aid an accident victim. They will stabilize the patient and transport her to a hospital for further care.

EMTs also deal with extremely stressful situations. Their actions can mean life or death for their patients. Patients can sometimes be violent or mentally unstable. EMTs may be exposed to transferable diseases, such as AIDS and hepatitis B. For an EMT, these kinds of problems are all in a day's work.

Why Do People Become EMTs?

Some people are interested in medicine but are not ready to spend years training to become a doctor. They may decide to train and work as an EMT as a first step. They can see how they like this kind of work before they commit to advanced study in the medical field. Some people know from personal experience just how important the work of an EMT is. Perhaps someone they know needed emergency care and received help from an EMT. Or perhaps they needed help themselves. They go on to become EMTs because they have seen the impact this kind of work can have on people's lives. They want to make a difference in their communities.

Training and Education

An EMT must be trained and certified. A person must have a high school diploma to enter an EMT training program. There are three levels of EMT training: EMT basic, EMT intermediate, and EMT paramedic. All EMTs learn how to use a backboard and stretcher. They are taught to deal with bleeding and fractures. They find out how to assist with an emergency childbirth. They are trained to recognize medical symptoms, such as those of cardiac arrest. An EMT paramedic is the highest level of EMT training. A paramedic usually studies at a community or technical college for one to two years.

What Skills and Qualities Must an EMT Have?

- An interest in helping injured or traumatized patients
- Desire to work in a fast-paced environment
- A level head in emergency situations
- Bravery
- Sound judgment
- Ability to follow directions
- Good communication skills
- Physical strength and stamina
- Strong teamwork skills

EMTs move a patient who has been transported to a hospital by helicopter. The prompt response of an EMT can mean the difference between life and death.

Paramedics are qualified to administer drugs. They can interpret ECGs, or electrocardiograms, which monitor heart activity, and they can use other advanced equipment. A paramedic can perform an endotracheal intubation if a patient is unable to breathe. This means the paramedic inserts a tube through the patient's mouth and into the trachea, or windpipe, to keep the airway open.

An EMT must be certified in the state where she practices. She must pass both a written and practical exam. Each state requires a certain number of hours spent working under the supervision of trained EMTs in an emergency room or ambulance. It is typical for states to require EMTs to be recertified every two years. EMTs must have ongoing training in order to remain certified.

Surprising Fact

Many people think that when there is an emergency, an ambulance driver does not have to obey traffic laws. In reality, the laws vary from state to state. In most places, an ambulance driver is still expected to obey traffic laws, such as stopping at a red light.[3] Even in times of emergency, public safety remains a high priority.

Advancement Opportunities

EMTs can advance to become a supervisor, manager, or director of emergency services. Some EMTs pursue further medical training. They may become registered nurses, physician's assistants, or physicians. Some become dispatchers or EMT instructors. Others sell or market emergency medical equipment to medical facilities.

Job Growth and Salary Outlook

Job openings for EMTs are expected to grow rapidly over the next decade. EMT positions have been filled by volunteers in the past, especially in rural areas where calls are infrequent. Because of the amount of training required, it is becoming

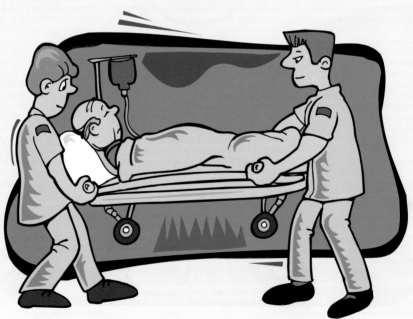

Choosing a Community Service Career

harder to find people willing to volunteer their time.[4] The middle 50 percent of EMTs earned $30,000 in 2009.[5] Workers with the highest levels of training will have the best job opportunities.

How Can I Learn More?

Call or visit a local hospital or nursing home. Ask if they have a volunteer program. Sign up for first aid and CPR classes.

Is This Career for You?

If you think you might be interested in being an EMT, think about the following questions:

- Do you thrive in fast-paced settings?

- Are you levelheaded in an emergency?

- Would you be able to kneel, lift, and carry heavy loads as a routine part of your job?

- When you hear sirens, do you want to rush to the scene to help?

- Are you able to make quick decisions?

- Would you like to help people who are injured?

- Are you good at working as part of a team?

Firefighters

Chapter 4

Facts About Firefighters

- Typical duties: responding to calls, putting out fires, performing acts of rescue and first aid, driving rescue vehicles, maintaining equipment, teaching public about fire safety and prevention, inspecting buildings to ensure they comply with fire codes, determining cause of a fire
- Average salary: $44,260[1]
- Skills needed: courage, endurance, initiative, sound judgment, physical strength and agility, teamwork skills
- Work environment: extremely hazardous conditions
- Schedule: often long shifts with irregular schedules

Most firefighters work for local fire departments. They put out fires and rescue any people in harm's way. Firefighters can also assist those in need of medical assistance. A firefighter is trained to provide basic emergency medical care. Firefighters also work in wilderness areas, fighting wildfires.

Firefighters work under extremely hazardous conditions, risking their lives.

A Day in the Life

Since a fire can break out at any time of the day or night, a firefighter may work long and irregular hours. Some work the entire twenty-four hours of one day. Then they get two days off. Others work long day or night shifts. While at the fire station, the firefighters are on alert at all times. They wear heavy, fire-retardant gear so they can be ready to go when a call comes in. The gear protects them from heat and flames at the scene of a fire. While waiting for a call, the firefighters clean and maintain the equipment. They practice fire drills to fine tune their skills. They complete paperwork and prepare reports on the fires they have attended. They work with the public to educate people about fire safety and prevention. They may read about new developments in firefighting or learn how to use new equipment.

When a call comes in, the firefighters must be ready to go. They grab their helmets and boots and board the fire trucks. They determine the fastest route to the fire and the nearest fire hydrant or water source. Once at the scene, the firefighters follow the direction of their fire chief. In this dangerous line of work, it is essential that they work together well as a team. They must get along and communicate well together to succeed. One firefighter uncoils a hose from the pumper truck. Several others work together to attach a hose from the pumper truck to a fire hydrant. Using the high-pressure hoses, they attack the fire with water and

Firefighters relax in the station. It is important that firefighters get along and communicate well to work as a team.

fire-retardant chemicals. The firefighters use ladders to gain better access to the flames. A firefighter cannot be afraid of heights. Using axes, they create vent holes in the roof of the building. This allows any trapped gases to escape. Otherwise, the gases can build up inside the building, causing it to explode. Firefighters enter burning buildings to rescue people inside. They perform emergency first aid. Firefighters do their best to secure nearby structures from the fire. They salvage personal property.

Benefits and Drawbacks

Most firefighters earn a good salary with health insurance and paid sick time. They may retire after twenty-five years of service. When they retire, they continue to receive a pension, sometimes equal to half their annual earnings.[2] Firefighters often earn extra money, above and beyond their salary, when they work more than their scheduled number of hours. This is called working overtime. Jobs in this field are very secure. Communities recognize the need for firefighters. These positions are unlikely to be cut in an attempt to balance the budget.[3] However, there is a reason why fire departments offer their workers such good benefits. Firefighters work under extremely dangerous conditions. They risk serious injury or death in the line of work. They are also exposed to hazardous chemicals and gases.

Why Do People Become Firefighters?

Firefighters take pride in providing a public service. They may be drawn to the excitement of a dangerous work environment. Firefighters can earn good salaries with excellent benefits.

Training and Education

To become a firefighter, you must have a high school diploma or GED, and you must be at least eighteen years old. Some college experience is preferred. Colleges offer both two-year and four-year degrees in fire science and engineering. Firefighters must pass written and physical exams to be considered for a job. The physical exam tests for stamina, strength, and agility. They also undergo a medical exam and drug testing. An important part of a firefighter's job is to provide first aid at the scene of a fire. All firefighters are trained EMTs. Once hired, firefighters usually attend several weeks of intensive training at a local fire academy. Firefighters continue to learn on the job from experienced coworkers. They attend workshops to stay up-to-date in firefighting and first-aid techniques.

Firefighters in protective gear get ready to go to a fire. Heavy protective clothing and equipment help keep firefighters safe.

Choosing a Community Service Career

What Skills and Qualities Must a Firefighter Have?

- Physical fitness
- Bravery
- Teamwork skills
- Ability to follow orders
- Organization
- Caution in dangerous situations
- Ability to make sound decisions under stress
- Dependability and responsibility
- Hardworking
- Willingness to work under hazardous conditions

Advancement Opportunities

To advance his career, a firefighter needs to pursue further knowledge. He may take classes at a community college to learn more about fire science. He may study building construction. A firefighter may train beyond EMT basic and become a paramedic. A fire chief needs to be comfortable speaking in public, managing staff, and working with budgets. The United States National Fire Academy offers a fire officer certification program.

A firefighter who demonstrates leadership qualities can advance within the department. He may be promoted to fire lieutenant, fire captain, or fire chief, or may leave the front

An entry-level firefighter needs to have college-level academic ability. Classes at the fire academy are equal to freshman-level college work.[4]

lines to work as a fire inspector. An inspector's job is to prevent fires. He examines buildings to ensure they meet the fire safety standards set by law. Another option is to become a fire investigator. A fire investigator tries to determine how a fire began and if it was arson, the act of setting a fire on purpose. An investigator may work for a fire or police department. Insurance companies also hire investigators to research claims.

Job Growth and Salary Outlook

The U.S. Department of Labor predicts that there will be an increase in firefighting jobs over the next decade. Many firefighters, especially in rural areas, are volunteers. As it gets harder to find qualified volunteers, towns will need to hire more professional firefighters.[5] Jobs in this field are popular. Candidates will need to be very well trained to compete.

Is This Career for You?

If you are thinking about becoming a firefighter, ask yourself the following questions:

- Do you like to play team sports?

- Do you accept directions easily?

- Do you communicate well with others?

- Do you lead a physically active lifestyle?

- Are you comfortable climbing ladders and entering enclosed spaces?

- Can people depend on you?

- Are you able to remain calm under stress?

Chapter 5

Social Workers

Facts About Social Workers

- Typical duties: helping people overcome difficulties, listening to and counseling clients, matching clients up with appropriate services
- Average salary: $39,530[1]
- Skills needed: open-minded and accepting nature, ability to listen, strong problem-solving skills
- Basic interests: assisting and guiding people in need
- Work environment: indoor office work, sometimes visiting people in their homes

When a person is going through a difficult time in life, it always helps to talk about it. A social worker can help simply by listening and asking questions. Once she understands what the issue is, a social worker can advise her client. Together they can take steps to begin to solve the problem. She may teach her client some skills to use, or she might recommend a resource or a program. Some social workers help people who are sick or have medical problems. Others work with people who have mental health or substance abuse issues. Many social workers help families and children.

A Day in the Life

Jennifer Stone is a social worker in a school system. Her schedule follows the school calendar. Public school is an ideal place for a social worker to reach out to children. She can help those students who are dealing with trouble in their personal lives.

Each school day, Stone is available to meet with the students, parents, and school staff. For example, she might meet one-on-one with a student who is acting out in class. She can help the student understand his emotions and help him to process them in an appropriate way. She may learn that the student is going through a difficult time at home. She can counsel the student and his family. She may refer them to an outside agency that can give them further support. She also collaborates with teachers and parents who are dealing with children with behavioral problems.

A school should be a place where people feel safe. A social worker works with the staff to foster a caring environment at the school. She works as a team with teachers, the principal, and other staff to set ground rules about what behaviors will not be tolerated. She assists the teachers in recognizing and rewarding

A social worker counsels a young woman. Social workers can help their clients take steps to resolve difficulties.

Choosing a Community Service Career

good behavior. A school social worker works to prevent teasing and bullying. She teaches the students to speak up if they see someone being teased or bullied. She also helps kids to learn how to handle bullying behavior if it happens to them.

An important part of a school social worker's job is to teach life skills. These tools will help the students to succeed in school and beyond. To this end, a social worker spends time with students in the classroom. She may read a picture book to elementary school children about feeling angry. Then she asks them to tell her about a time when they have felt angry and how they resolved it. She has the children practice using words to express their emotions. The teacher can build on this lesson by using this language during the rest of the school year.

Stone strives to give the students the support they need so they may do well in school. She teaches the children how to handle difficult situations appropriately. The students appreciate her respect and support.

Benefits and Drawbacks

Because a social worker helps people to solve difficult life problems, the work can be very rewarding emotionally. Jennifer Stone says, "Witnessing a student handle a situation appropriately, using the skills we've practiced together, is exciting."[2] On the down side, social workers deal with life's most disturbing situations. And there is only so much a social worker can do. For this reason, the job can be emotionally draining.

A social worker speaks with a father and his daughter. One of
a social worker's greatest skills is listening.

Choosing a Community Service Career

Why Do People Become Social Workers?

Social workers believe that, with support, people can change their lives for the better. Social workers are good at listening to people. They do not judge what they hear, but listen with an open mind. They approach tough situations as problems that can be solved. Social workers feel gratified when they help people to reach their full potential.

Training and Education

Jobs in this field require at least a four-year bachelor's degree in social work or a related field, such as counseling or psychology. An accredited bachelor's degree in social work requires four hundred hours of supervised field experience. A social worker with this degree earns the title of licensed social worker, or LSW. Positions often require an additional two-year master's degree. At the highest levels, social workers need to obtain a doctorate degree (PhD). Most states require social workers to be certified and licensed by the state. State license boards require ongoing training so that social workers maintain a current knowledge of the field. The National Association of Social Workers provides national certification.

What Skills and Qualities Must a Social Worker Have?

- Ability to empathize with people
  A wish to help improve the lives of others
- Good communication skills, especially listening
- A sense of optimism
  An understanding of emotions and how they influence people's actions
- Desire to work with people, both one-on-one and in group settings
- Accepting attitude toward others
  Strong problem-solving skills
- Interest in social behavior
- Time-management skills

Advancement Opportunities

A social worker can advance within the agency where she works. She can become a supervisor, manager, or director. A social worker with a master's degree may open her own private practice.

Social workers help people of all ages with many kinds of problems.

Surprising Fact

Stone was amazed at the wide range of issues with which students must cope. The children need help with behavior issues, such as bullying. Students may come to her when they have trouble at home. Their parents may be going through a divorce or a separation. She also sees children who are suffering from very serious issues, such as neglect and abuse.

Job Growth and Salary Outlook

Jobs in this field are projected to grow faster than those in other fields.[3] As the baby-boom generation ages, the growing number of senior citizens will require assistance. Better understanding of alcohol and drug abuse will lead to more support programs. The number of children with special needs is also on the rise. These children and their families will require the help of social workers. There will be more jobs for social workers in rural areas. Salary depends on various factors, such as the level of education, type of social work, the region, and the employer. In 2006, the middle 50 percent of social workers earned between $31,040 and $52,080.[4]

Choosing a Community Service Career

How Can I Learn More?

Talk with your school guidance counselor about your interest. Sign up for as many classes as you can in the social sciences. Look for opportunities to help others in your community. If your school or church offers peer support groups, sign up to take part. Volunteer in community activities that interest you.

Is This Career for You?

If you are thinking about being a social worker, ask yourself these questions:

- Do you believe people can improve their lives if they have the right skills and support?

- Do people come to you when they have a problem or need to talk?

- Are you emotionally mature?

- Can you keep a secret when information is told to you in confidence?

- Are you open-minded and accepting of differences?

- Are you good at finding solutions to problems?

- Do you have a strong desire to help people in need?

Teachers

Facts About Teachers

- Typical duties: helping students to learn new information and skills, maintaining discipline and order in the classroom, creating lesson plans, assigning and grading work, assessing each student's needs
- Average salary: $50,950[1]
- Skills needed: patience, ability to convey information to all different types of learners, ability to multitask, a sense of fairness, consistency, problem-solving skills
- Basic interests: love of learning, interest in children and their development
- Work environment: indoors, often as the only adult in a classroom of children

A teacher's job is to help students learn new skills. He provides the students with opportunities to grow. He assesses each student's level of learning and helps them to meet both state and federal standards for education.

Teaching is a good career for those who enjoy sharing their knowledge with others.

A teacher is responsible for preparing lesson plans and filling out required paperwork. He spends most of the school day in the classroom, instructing students.

A Day in the Life

Stacey Augustine is a kindergarten teacher who works at a public elementary school. Each morning, she comes to school early and looks over her lesson plans for the day. She completes any last-minute preparations. She may need to make photocopies or get together materials for a craft project. Sometimes she attends a meeting with other teachers.

When the students arrive, the teacher takes attendance and reads over any notes from her students' parents while the children sign in. Next she has the children sit for circle time, and she explains what their day will be like. In the morning, they will work on their math skills. She divides the students into small groups. She assigns each group to one of the stations she has set up around the room. Each station is a table where the students will work on a math activity. The children often use tools such as board games to help them learn in a fun and engaging way. The teacher moves from station to station, assisting the children if they need guidance.

When time is up, the children help to clear the tables and then line up to wash their hands. The teacher passes out a nutritious snack provided by the school. Now it is time for them to walk down the hall to the school library. The librarian will read to the children. The teacher may use this time to fill out some paperwork. The state requires teachers to maintain detailed records. The students go to the library once a week. Other days of the week they have gym, music, art, or computer time. Each of these specialized classes is taught by a different teacher.

At lunchtime, the children eat in the cafeteria. Augustine uses this time to help an older child at the school who is having difficulty learning to read. After lunch, the children have an outdoor recess so they can get some fresh air and exercise. The teacher sets up the afternoon activities. She will work with the students on their literacy skills. By the end of the school year, each of her students will be reading on his or her own. When they begin the year, most of them do not know how to read at all. When the recess bell rings, the students return to the classroom. They sit quietly while their teacher reads them a story. Then they take turns reading and spelling words on the dry erase board.

When a child keeps talking out of turn, the teacher kindly asks the student to raise his hand so that she may call on him before he speaks. She is consistent with her expectations for her students. She tells them how proud she is when they make good choices. They work hard to please her. At the end of the day, the teacher has the children neaten the classroom together. They gather up their things and wait in line. They may sing a song together while they wait. The bell rings and the students head out to the bus lines or meet their parents. Augustine looks over her lesson plans for the rest of the week to determine what work she needs to bring home. Although school is out for the students at three o'clock in the afternoon, most teachers must bring their work home with them.

Why Do People Become Teachers?

Teachers are people who love to learn and see the value of learning new information. Teachers really enjoy sharing knowledge with their students. They are thrilled when a

In addition to the task of managing a classroom, a teacher needs to handle large amounts of paperwork, such as planning lessons, grading papers, and evaluating students.

student suddenly sees how it all fits together and says "A-ha!" Teachers understand that by helping children to learn new skills, they are shaping the course of the child's life. They take satisfaction in providing children with opportunities to excel and fulfill their potential.

Benefits and Drawbacks

Teachers are very busy during the school day. While many like this fast pace, teachers work more than forty hours a week because they must take work home with them. Some people are attracted to the schedule. Many teachers have two months off in the summer. Of course, this can also be a drawback as it may force them to find alternative work for part of the year. The toughest challenges teachers may face occur

Choosing a Community Service Career

in underfunded schools. When there are not enough funds, there are more students per teacher. Supplies are inadequate and the facilities may be in disrepair. The students are also coping with the stresses of poverty in their daily lives. As a result, they may be unruly, disrespectful, and even violent at times.

What Skills and Qualities Must a Teacher Have?

- Enthusiasm for learning
- Desire to help others achieve
- Patience
- Caring and empathy toward all children
- Sense of fairness and ability to be consistent
- Flexibility
- Ability to think on your feet
- Creativity
- Strong organizational skills
- Sense of humor

Teachers get satisfaction from helping students master new skills.

Choosing a Community Service Career

Training and Education

Teachers must be certified by a state licensing board. Each state requires at least a four-year degree, with a core of education courses. The license requirements vary depending on the grade level. Teachers may be certified to teach at the elementary school, middle school, or secondary school level. Secondary school teachers usually need degrees in the area of study they will teach, such as history. All teachers must complete a period of student teaching under the supervision of a licensed teacher.

Some states require that teachers either have, or work toward, a further two-year master's degree in education. School districts often pay part or all of their teachers' further education costs. Teachers with higher degrees earn higher salaries. To maintain their licenses, teachers need to continue to take educational workshops and ongoing training.

Advancement Opportunities

Some school districts promote good teachers to act as lead or head teachers. In addition to their classroom responsibilities, they support and guide new teachers. A teacher who wants to advance her career may go back to school to learn more. Then she can apply for a job such as a curriculum adviser, school librarian, or as a specialist in technology, math, or literacy. Other teachers leave the classroom altogether and move into administrative positions such as school principal.

Job Growth and Salary Outlook

Large numbers of teachers will retire wihin the next decade.[2] Areas experiencing a boom in population growth will need the most new teachers.[3] Teachers who specialize in mathematics, chemistry, physics, and foreign languages will find the most job openings. Having a master's degree improves a teacher's chances of finding work, too. Salaries for public school elementary and secondary school teachers average $41,400 to $45,920 annually. However, starting salaries are often much lower. Preschool teachers, too, often have lower earnings. The average salary for a preschool teacher in 2008 was $23,870.[4]

How Can I Learn More?

Spend as much time as you can in classrooms. Work with different ages of children to determine what ages you enjoy working with most. Look for opportunities to work with them outside of a classroom, too. A good teacher appreciates children and their interests. Learn as much as you can about a wide variety of subjects to help students make connections.

Is This Career for You?

Are you thinking about being a teacher? Ask yourself these questions:

- Do you enjoy learning new things?

- Do you feel comfortable working with children?

- Are you a creative person?

- Are you open-minded and accepting of different types of people?

- Are you good at sharing your enthusiasm for learning?

- Are you able to think on your feet and handle situations as they arise?

- Do you find it rewarding to help someone learn something new?

Chapter 7

Clergypeople

Facts About Clergypeople

- Typical duties: providing spiritual care, guidance, and leadership to a congregation; leading worship services; visiting with those who are sick, shut-in, or in need; listening and counseling; performing important ceremonies such as weddings and funerals
- Median annual salary: $42,950[1]
- Skills needed: strong leadership ability, public speaking, and emotional maturity
- Basic interests: deep commitment to one's religious faith and a desire to share that faith
- Work environment: working with many different kinds of people, both one-on-one and in a group setting; public speaking

A clergyperson—whether a Protestant minister, Catholic priest, Jewish rabbi, Muslim imam, or other religious leader—supports and counsels people. As the leader of a church, temple,

A Protestant minister and choir members. Clergypeople work with a number of different groups in planning services.

or mosque, a minister gives spiritual guidance to the people of the congregation. A minister seeks to help people grow in their faith. A minister may be a community activist who speaks up for the rights of the poor and the ill.

A Day in the Life

Laura Holt-Haslam is an ordained minister. She works as a pastor at an urban church with a small but growing congregation. It is her job to offer support and spiritual guidance to the people of her church. She strives to use her talents and skills to serve others. She encourages the people of her church to do this, too. She plans and leads weekly worship services and Bible study groups. She visits members of the congregation who are in need. This may be someone recuperating from surgery in the hospital, an elderly shut-in, or someone grieving the recent loss of a loved one. She talks with them and listens to their concerns. She offers prayer, counsel, and her support.

A minister performs important ceremonies, such as baptisms, weddings, and funerals. She works with church leaders to oversee the church's programs. Sometimes pastors are community activists, attending to the needs of the poor or marginalized in the wider society. For instance, a minister may organize a soup kitchen for the homeless, an after-school program for the underprivileged, or free clothes for those who need them. A minister encourages and trains people to use their skills and strengths to serve others.

Clergy of all faiths engage in teaching. Here a rabbi meets with students getting ready for their Bar Mitzvah and Bat Mitzvah ceremonies.

Benefits and Drawbacks

A minister's work is highly rewarding. Clergypeople have the satisfaction of seeing people grow in their faith. She helps people to serve and strengthen their communities. A minister's work is varied. One day a minister may be presiding over a wedding. The next she might work with a youth group, helping them to strengthen their faith. On the down side, a minister may feel pressure to be perfect. Of course, ministers are people, too, and people are far from perfect. Ministers must please the many different people in their congregation, as well as follow their own calling. This balancing act can be a challenge.

Most clergy jobs do not pay terribly well, though some include housing and a car allowance. Some ministers can find only part-time work. However, a minister's work is never done. When a member of the congregation needs support, a minister feels compelled to help.

An imam speaks to worshippers at a mosque in Florida. Preaching is one of the main duties of the clergy.

What Skills and Qualities Must a Clergyperson Have?

- Deep religious faith
- Desire to serve people
- Concern and empathy
- Strong listening skills
- Ability to motivate and inspire people
- Public speaking skills
- Leadership ability
- Problem-solving and conflict-resolution skills
- Wish to bring about positive changes

Why Do People Become Ministers?

Clergypeople believe that they are fulfilling a call from God. They have a strong religious faith that guides their actions. They are leaders who have a desire to make a difference in the world. Ministers take great satisfaction in helping others to grow spiritually. Holt-Haslam states: "I like knowing that I have encouraged and helped a person through a difficult time and have made a positive difference in his or her life."[2]

Training and Education

Most denominations require that a minister is ordained. To be ordained, a person must study at a seminary, also called theological college or divinity school, for three years to obtain a master's degree. Next he or she completes an internship at a church or other ministry. Then the candidate prepares a paper about his journey of faith and his beliefs. He must present and defend his paper before a group of clergy. Once this process is complete, a minister may be ordained. Small churches may have lay ministers who work as volunteers. A lay minister is not ordained and typically works at another full-time job to support himself.

Advancement Opportunities

Different denominations have varying levels of leadership roles within the church. A large church may employ many ministers. As a minister gains experience, he often takes on more responsibilities. A minister might not consider personal advancement as a career goal. A minister's work is guided by a strong faith in God. A minister may feel called to serve God in many ways. The next step in a minister's career may not be a step up on the pay scale. Ministers often meet together with other clergy to share ideas and foster community. There are many workshops available for clergy to further develop their skills.

Job Growth and Salary Outlook

There will always be a need for spiritual leaders. People who choose this path in life can bring about great change, both in the lives of the individuals they care for and in the larger community. The U.S. Department of Labor forecasts the growth rate for jobs in the clergy to be average over the next decade.[3] Ministers who work for private companies can expect to earn significantly higher salaries than those working for nonprofit organizations, such as churches.[4]

Surprising Fact

A clergyperson needs to be self-motivated. One new minister was surprised at how much independence he had to create his own schedule. After the structure of his schooling, this took some getting used to.[5]

How Can I Learn More?

Get involved in your church. Talk with your minister about your interest. Ask if you can assist in leading worship. Take part in youth leadership activities at your church. Attend or work at a church summer camp. Learn as much as you can about your faith's traditions. Look for opportunities to use your strengths and talents to serve people in need. Pray and seek divine guidance.

Is This Career for You?

If you are contemplating a career in the clergy, think about these questions:

- Do you feel a strong connection with God?

- Do you feel comfortable and at home in your place of worship?

- Do you enjoy working with all kinds of people?

- Would you like to help others find spiritual fulfillment?

- Would you feel comfortable speaking in front of large groups?

- Do you like to spend time in quiet prayer, contemplation, and study?

- Do you want to make a difference in the world?

Chapter 8

Librarians

Facts About Librarians

- Typical duties: helping people to find information; buying, organizing, and cataloging books, magazines, and other materials
- Average salary: $52,530[1]
- Skills needed: strong communication skills, in particular reading and writing; organizational skills; and computer skills
- Basic interests: reading, doing research, helping people, working with computers
- Work environment: indoor setting, often working with public

A librarian helps people who come to the library in search of information. A library houses a collection of books and other print materials, and computers for patrons to use. Using the Internet, people can access information from all around the world. A librarian helps patrons use computers and find materials on the shelf.

A librarian helps patrons find the materials they need. If you enjoy helping people get information, you might like to work in a library.

A Day in the Life

Melanie Taylor works in a public library in a town with a population of seven thousand. As the director of the library, she has a wide range of responsibilities. She oversees a small staff of library workers and interns. She recruits and trains volunteers. She keeps the library's collection up-to-date. She reads reviews of newly published books and decides what to purchase. When new material arrives, the books are cataloged and prepared for display. She removes tattered or obsolete material from the shelves.

Her job as library director goes well beyond caring for books. She must oversee the maintenance of the historic building that houses the library's collection. If the copier or other equipment breaks down, she calls the repair technician. She must also make plans for the future of the library: What information will people need and how can the library provide it? She uses her writing skills to apply for grant money to help fund the library. She develops the annual budget. Despite all these tasks, one can often find her at the front desk. She greets patrons and helps them to locate books. Like all good librarians, she is friendly and easy to approach. A librarian, by nature, puts the needs of others before her own.[2]

Taylor faces such a wide array of tasks because she works at a small, rural library. In a larger library, there are more people on staff to share the workload. Their jobs are more specialized and may be split into departments. A librarian might focus exclusively on acquiring new titles. Another may develop programs to encourage early literacy for children. Someone else could work at the reference desk, helping patrons in their search for information.

Choosing a Community Service Career

An administrative librarian might prepare budgets and oversee the work of the departments. Library assistants and library technicians also work at a library. These jobs require less training and do not pay as well.

Benefits and Drawbacks to the Job

A librarian works with information, from facts to ideas. He is always learning something new. He can amass a wide body of knowledge during the course of his career. The job can vary greatly from one day to the next. This may appeal to a person who likes to face new challenges. It is a drawback for someone who depends on the stability of routine. Librarians spend a lot of time seated at a desk. Working with computers can cause eyestrain and wrist problems. For many librarians, helping the public is a rewarding part of the job. However, it can be a source of stress, too. This is particularly true in a corporate library, when the patron is facing a looming deadline.

Why People Choose to Become Librarians

People who go into this field love to read, do research, and learn new things. They enjoy working with people, helping them to make connections and find information.

A librarian returns books to the shelf. The library staff is responsible for keeping books organized and accessible.

Choosing a Community Service Career

Librarians share their love of reading with others. They promote literacy in their community. They are also highly organized and good at solving problems.

Required Training and Education

Most jobs in this field require a four-year bachelor's degree, and then a one- to two-year master's degree in library or information science. Those who wish to work in a specialized library may need additional education. For instance, a job in a law library would require knowledge of the legal system. All librarians are expected to be up-to-date on the latest advances in information science. This can be a tough challenge. The field has undergone rapid changes in recent years.

What Skills and Qualities Does a Librarian Need?

- Love of reading
- Friendly attitude and willingness to help others
- Good communication skills
- Knowledge of computers
- Ability and willingness to learn new technology
- Strong organizational skills
- Enjoyment of multitasking

Advancement Opportunities

A new librarian often starts at an entry-level position in a library. As she gains experience, she can move up through the ranks. She may be promoted to head a department. Higher-level positions usually involve more long-term planning and administrative tasks. A skilled librarian can become the executive director of a library.

Today's librarians have to be computer savvy.

Job Growth and Salary Outlook

The Bureau of Labor Statistics projects that jobs in this field will grow 8 percent over the next decade, which is just average growth. Many librarians work for a school, town, state, or the federal government. Tax dollars pay their salaries. As a way to cut costs for taxpayers, governments may hire fewer highly skilled librarians. Instead, they may hire staff with less education and experience who will work for less pay. Already library assistants and technicians are doing work that used to require a master's of library science.[4] But that should not discourage you if this is your dream job. Two out of three librarians are over the age of forty-five.[5] Positions will open up in the field as these workers retire.

How Can I Learn More?

Taylor recommends that anyone interested in a career in library science "read, read, read, oh, and read."[6] Spend time at your school library. Visit your town library. Talk with the librarians about your interest. Ask about their career paths and get their advice. Look into volunteer programs at your library. Does your library not have a volunteer program? Talk with the librarian about starting one.

Is This Career for You?

Do you think you'd like to be a librarian? Think about the following questions:

- Do you love to read?

- Do you like spending time in libraries?

- Do you like finding information on a computer?

- Do you like learning new ways to use computers?

- Are you good at listening to people?

- Do you recommend books to your friends?

- Would you enjoy assisting people who are looking for information?

- Do you like solving complex problems?

- Would you like working as a member of a team?

- Do you feel proud when you are able to help someone?

Choosing a Community Service Career

Child-Care Workers

Chapter 9

Facts About Child-Care Workers

- Typical duties: caring for infants, toddlers, and preschool children while their parents are at work
- Median annual salary: $20,940[1]
- Skills needed: patience and understanding of the needs of children at different age levels, knowledge of safety and care issues for infants and preschool children
- Basic interests: helping children to grow and learn in a safe and welcoming environment
- Work environment: at the child's home, at the caregiver's home, or at a separate child-care facility.
- Schedule: often long hours, although many work part-time

A child-care worker cares for children while their parents are at work. Some work in a day-care facility, while others care for children in their homes. A nanny or au pair typically lives with the family for whom she works. Room and board (lodging and meals) may be part of her salary.

85

A Day in the Life

Many child-care workers are employed as part of a team in a day-care facility. As the children arrive for the day, a child-care worker greets them and makes them feel welcome. She assists them in their transition to day care. For some kids, this can be a difficult time. She may engage a child in an activity to take his mind off any anxiety about separating from his parents.

This woman cares for several children in her home. Other child-care workers are in day-care centers.

Choosing a Community Service Career

A child-care worker needs to be creative and know what will interest children. She spends much of her time creating activities for the children to do. They must be suitable for each child's age and ability level. One of the most rewarding parts of the job is helping the children to learn new skills. She may encourage a baby to roll over to reach a new toy, or teach a preschooler how to grasp a pencil correctly. Preschool children are ready to learn pre-reading and early math skills. She may work with them to learn the sounds of the alphabet and to recognize letters and numbers.

Exercise and fresh air are important parts of a healthy childhood. Children need to spend time each day playing outdoors. A child-care worker may take children for a walk and point things out to them. Many child-care facilities have playground equipment for the children to play on. While they run, hop, and roll a ball back and forth, the children are developing their gross motor skills. Children need a lot of food to keep up with all the energy they expend. A child-care worker provides healthy snacks and meals. All children need time to rest during the day, too. Day-care centers have a designated time for the children to nap or rest quietly.

Young children learn through play.

Choosing a Community Service Career

A child-care worker shows children how to behave. She models good behavior for them. She teaches them social skills, such as how to share and be polite. She teaches the children how to communicate their emotions. When a young child is frustrated, he may kick or scream to express himself. Children need help learning how to express their emotions using words. A child-care worker is constantly teaching children which behaviors are acceptable. She must be patient and consistent.

Sometimes a child-care worker watches older children before and after their school day. At the end of the day, she may greet the children at the bus stop, provide a snack, and encourage the children to complete their homework before going out to play. A child-care worker can also care for an infant. Infants require constant care. They must be fed, burped, diapered, comforted, played with, and put down for naps. Most states have strict laws about the number of infants that a child-care worker can watch.

A child-care worker needs to be able to communicate clearly, and not just with kids. She must talk often with the children's parents. They need to know how their child is doing and how they can help to meet their child's needs.

Child-Care Workers

Benefits and Drawbacks

Child-care workers generally do not earn much money. However, there are exceptions: for instance, a worker who runs her own successful child-care center may do well. Working with children is very rewarding and fun. It can be also exhausting, both physically and emotionally. Children do well with a regular daily routine, but this can be a drawback for adults who like a more varied schedule.

Why Do People Become Child-Care Workers?

Child-care workers love to spend time with children. They take pride in helping their young charges to learn and grow. Some are stay-at-home parents. They want to work but are unwilling to take a job that would take them away from their family. They decide to make a career out of child rearing, and they watch other people's children, too.

Required Training and Education

It is possible to go into this field with just a high school diploma. Employers look for hands-on experience with children. Some of the higher-paying jobs in this field require a two- or four-year degree in early childhood education. CPR/first-aid training is always an asset and often a requirement.

A child-care worker's top priority is safety. In most states, a child-care worker does not need a license to get a job unless she is self-employed. Instead, states require child-care centers to be licensed. To meet the license requirements, child-care workers at the center may need to pass a background check.[2]

Advancement Opportunities

In a child-care center, a worker can advance to a managerial or administrative position. A child-care worker may pursue further education and become a preschool or elementary school teacher. She may open her own child-care facility and take on the challenges of running a small business. She may leave the field and pursue different interests once her own children are grown.

Job Growth and Salary Outlook

The job outlook is very good. The number of working parents and children under the age of five is projected to rise over the next decade.[3] Jobs will open up as current workers leave to find a less demanding job with better pay. Salaries are generally quite low. The average child-care worker in 2009 made just $20,940 a year.[4] However, a flexible schedule is a key benefit for some people. Many child-care workers choose to work only part- time. This leaves them time to pursue other interests, such as attending college.

What Skills and Qualities Must a Child-Care Worker Have?

- Desire to work with babies and young children
- Patience and consistency
- Ability to work on a team
- Ability to model good behavior and choices
- Physical strength and stamina to lift and carry children
- Good communication skills, both with children and their parents/guardians
- Knowledge of childhood safety and health issues
- Ability to provide constant, focused attention
- Ability to stay calm in an emergency situation
- Desire to help children learn and grow

Choosing a Community Service Career

Interest in nurturing young children is an important quality for child-care workers. Babysitting can help you decide whether this career is for you.

How Can I Learn More?

Look for opportunities to work with children. If you have a younger brother or sister, you may have already gotten a feel for it. Perhaps a relative or family friend needs a babysitter, but make sure you are ready for the responsibility. You can also try contacting a day-care facility in your area. Ask if you can come in to get a tour or volunteer.

Is This Career for You?

If you think you'd like to be a child-care worker, ask yourself the following questions:

- Do you like to read stories and play games with children?

- Do you have a friendly and upbeat personality?

- Can you bend, lift, and carry up to 50 pounds as part of a daily routine?

- Are you vigilant and watchful for potentially dangerous situations?

- Do you keep a cool head in an emergency?

- Do you like to take care of infants?

- Do you enjoy helping children to learn new skills?

Postal Workers

Chapter 10

Facts About Postal Workers

- Typical duties: sorts, delivers, and collects letters and packages; interacts with the public
- Average salary: $49,800[1]
- Skills needed: attention to detail, ability to communicate well with the public, ability to lift up to 70 lbs.
- Basic interests: interacting with the public, providing a community service
- Work environment: varied—outdoors, behind the wheel of a delivery vehicle, at a service counter, or in a warehouse

The U.S. Postal Service hires people to sort, carry, and distribute mail throughout the nation. Some employees assist customers at a post office. Others work in mail-processing centers. They operate machines that sort the mail. Some drive trucks that carry the mail to the town where it is going. Mail carriers walk or drive along a route, delivering mail.

Many people enjoy working for the U.S. Postal Service because they
have an opportunity to help people.

Choosing a Community Service Career

A Day in the Life

A rural mail carrier sorts mail into the order it will be delivered. She loads mail into her own car. The postal service reimburses her for the mileage she puts on her car while delivering the mail. The steering wheel has been moved to the right side of the vehicle so she can reach mailboxes from her car window. She attaches a sign to the top of her car that reads "U.S. Mail." An orange triangle affixed to the left side of her car alerts other drivers that she will be making frequent stops. Along her delivery route, she stops at each mailbox to deliver letters and packages. When the flag is up on a mailbox, she collects the mail inside. At the end of her route, she will return to the post office and drop off the mail she has collected. If a package will not fit in a mailbox, she drives up to the customer's home to deliver it in person.

It may require a signature from the person who is receiving it. If the person is not at home, she leaves a slip in the mailbox. The slip tells the person where they can pick up the package. She collects money for mail if there is postage due or if it has been sent C.O.D.: cash-on-delivery. Like all rural mail

A customer signs for a package at a post office at Holloman
Air Force Base in Alamogordo, New Mexico. Many postal
workers help the public directly.

Choosing a Community Service Career

carriers, she can provide customers on her route with additional mail services. She sells stamps and money orders. She provides forms for people who are moving and need to notify the post office of their new address. When a person is going away on vacation, he can request a form to alert the post office. They will hold his mail until he returns.

Benefits and Drawbacks

Jobs with the federal government are very secure. Workers receive excellent benefits. They can count on steady pay increases. All this, and there is no expensive training or schooling needed. As a result, these jobs are very competitive. Applicants must first take a civil service test. If they do well on the test, they are eligible to apply for a job opening. It is not unusual to have to wait one or even two years after the test before being hired.[2] The work can be repetitive. While some workers enjoy the daily routine, others might grow bored.

Why Do People Become Postal Workers?

Postal workers take pride in performing an important public service. They are responsible and pay careful attention to detail. Postal carriers and clerks need to be friendly and courteous. A large part of their job is helping the public.

Training and Education

A person must be a citizen of the United States or have permanent resident-alien status to work for the Postal Service. There are no educational requirements to work in this field, but a person must be at least eighteen years old. To apply for a Postal Service job, a person signs up to take a civil service exam. Applicants can buy study guides to help them prepare. The exam tests a person's ability to read accurately and quickly and determines the person's skill at memorizing regulations. Those with a score of at least 70 percent are put on a list. The higher a person's score, the better his chance of employment. Honorably discharged veterans receive five extra points. Disabled veterans receive ten extra points. When a job becomes available, the postmaster contacts people from the top of the list and interviews them for the job. The exam scores are good for two years. Then the test results expire. Applicants have to reapply by taking the exam again.

What Skills and Qualities Must a Postal Worker Have?

- Desire to serve people
- Pride in providing an important public service
- Attention to detail
- Ability to lift heavy loads
- Good memory
- Good communication skills
- Maturity and responsibility
- Ability to handle feedback
- Good interpersonal skills
- Fluent English

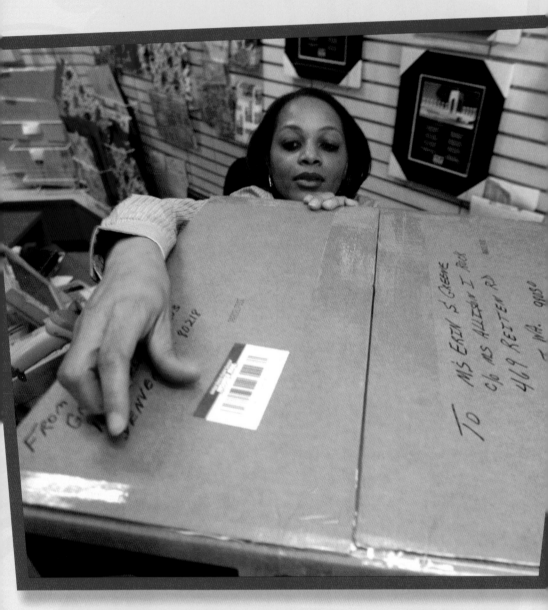

A postal service employee readies a holiday package for mailing. Postal workers need to be able to carry parcels weighing up to 70 pounds.

Choosing a Community Service Career

Mail carriers must hold a valid driver's license and have a safe driving record. If the job requires driving a vehicle, applicants must pass a road test. All postal workers must pass a physical exam before they begin work. They need to be able to lift and carry a 70-pound mailbag. They also must undergo drug testing. Experienced postal workers provide on-the-job training to newly hired workers.

Advancement Opportunities

When a shift or mail route opens up, postal workers can apply for it through a bidding process. Their chances depend on seniority—the length of time they have held their job. Postal workers can also advance to supervisory roles. For example, the current postmaster general started out as a window clerk at a post office.[3]

In addition to moving into supervisory roles, people can advance into different types of careers within the U.S. Postal Service. This giant organization hires people to do many kinds of work, not just to handle the mail. They need accountants and computer specialists. They have jobs in customer relations, advertising, and marketing.

Job Growth and Salary Outlook

Jobs for postal carriers and clerks are expected to stay steady over the next decade. There may even be fewer jobs in the future for mail processors and sorters. Sorting the mail has become more efficient with the help of computers. The increased use of e-mail and the Internet is also affecting the amount of mail people send. Jobs in this field will continue to be highly competitive. They are popular because the benefits are quite good and the entry requirements are minimal. The better qualified candidates will have the best opportunities. Veterans of the armed forces are given preference.

How Can I Learn More?

Check out the U.S. Postal Service's extensive Web site. Spend some time at your local post office. Find out if they offer job shadowing opportunities. If you are interested, look for a copy of the Postal Service exam study guide. This can give you a better understanding of what the civil service exam involves.

Is This Career for You?

If you think you'd like to be a postal worker, answer the following questions:

- Can you read quickly and accurately?

- Do you enjoy interacting with people?

- Do you like to have a daily routine?

- Are you friendly and courteous?

- Are you physically fit and able to carry up to 70 pounds?

- Are you detail oriented?

- Do you have a good memory?

Chapter 11

Funeral Directors

Facts About Funeral Directors

- Typical duties: working with grieving families to oversee details of funeral services and burials; transporting and preparing the deceased for viewings, burial, or cremation
- Median annual earnings: $52,210[1]
- Skills needed: excellent communication and interpersonal skills, ability to communicate respect and compassion, strong organizational skills, attention to detail
- Required interests: the funeral customs of different cultures, helping individuals who are coping with grief
- Work environment: varied settings, primarily indoors; working with the public; hazardous chemicals
- Schedule: often irregular or shift work—must be flexible

The death of a loved one throws a family into sadness and shock. During this highly emotional time, there are an overwhelming number of decisions that must be made. That is where a funeral director steps in to help. It is his job to guide the family through the process. In this way, a funeral director provides an invaluable service. He eases the burden on the family and allows them to take time to grieve.

A Day in the Life

Jeremy McFarlane is a funeral director in a rural area. He and his family own a funeral home. The schedule is hard to predict. The phone may ring at any time of the day or night. Days may go by without any calls. When he does get a call, it is his job to transport the body of the deceased to the funeral home. Using a collapsible cot, he removes the body from the place of death. He drives a hearse, a formal black car with space in the back

Funeral home directors are experienced at helping people who have lost a loved one, who need to be treated with sensitivity and respect.

to transport a casket. He talks with the family to determine what will be done next. Together they set a time and place for a memorial service or other funeral ceremony. He is familiar with the funeral traditions of the people in his community. For example, a family's religion may dictate how the body is laid to rest. Families may choose to have the deceased cremated. Cremation means the body is burned in a special furnace. The family is given the ashes, or cremains, that remain. They may choose to keep the ashes in an urn. They may bury or scatter them in a favorite spot.

Some families hold a wake or a viewing. These visiting hours are a time for friends and family to gather to pay their respects. Sometimes the body is embalmed for sanitary reasons. Using an embalming machine, the funeral director pumps embalming chemicals through the veins. The chemicals act to preserve the body. During this process the funeral director wears a respirator and protective gloves. A funeral director cannot be squeamish. Like a doctor or any other health professional, he must be able to handle trauma to bodies. He also cleans and dresses the body. It is his job to make the body look at peace and restful for the viewing. He may use makeup or cotton to achieve this effect.

A funeral director must be calm and composed. He has to handle many details without becoming flustered. He helps the family to select a casket or urn. He coordinates with the clergy who will perform the funeral ceremony. He arranges for pallbearers to carry the casket. He contacts the cemetery staff to arrange for the opening and closing of the burial plot, or he

A funeral director (at left) with the family of a young man killed in the war in Iraq. Funeral directors help see that the visitation, funeral, and burial ceremonies go smoothly.

arranges with a crematorium for the cremation. He prepares the viewing room and the flower arrangements at the memorial service. He may have employees to assist him with these tasks.

It is common for families to feel overwhelmed during this time. They may be unsure how they will cope without their loved one. Some funeral homes offer support groups for families. Other funeral homes help people by referring them to their clergy or social workers.

A funeral director keeps records and prepares invoices. He must also fill out a lot of paperwork. He files a death certificate with the state. He notifies the Social Security Administration.

He interviews the family so he can write an obituary for local newspapers. An obituary informs the public of a person's death. It tells the story of a person's life and the details of any memorial service. A funeral director may help families with other paperwork as well, such as forms for the transfer of pension funds or insurance policies. If the body will be buried out of state, additional paperwork is required.

A funeral director also works with people who want to arrange the details of their funeral in advance. People may want to communicate their own wishes for their funeral. Often they simply want to ease the burden on their families.

Why Do People Become Funeral Directors?

A funeral director likes helping others in times of need. He takes pride in his role as a community leader. He is a dependable and responsible person. He plays an essential and highly visible role in the community. In return, people respect his work and hold him in high esteem.

Benefits and Drawbacks

McFarlane takes personal satisfaction in his work. He is rewarded when people thank him for his help and guidance. "You must be comfortable with yourself," he states. "Interpersonal skills and the ability to form a bond with

Choosing a Community Service Career

What Skills and Qualities Does a Funeral Director Need?

- Patience
- Respect
- Ability to communicate clearly and tactfully
- Ability to remain calm under stress
- Ability to think on your feet
- Attention to detail
- Ability to calmly handle many tasks
- Strong organizational skills
- A clinical attitude toward trauma to bodies
- Desire to help people who are going through a difficult experience

people right away: these things are essential to the job."[2] He routinely helps people who are very sad and even in shock or denial over the death of their loved one. For this reason, the job can be emotionally taxing. Also, the hours are unpredictable as a death may occur at any given time, and he must be ready at a moment's notice to retrieve the body. Furthermore, funeral directors may be exposed to hazardous chemicals and infectious diseases.

Required Training and Education

Funeral directors obtain a two- or four-year degree in mortuary science. They complete an apprenticeship under the guidance of a licensed funeral director. Then they may apply for a license from the state. The license requires them to pass both a practical and a written test. The license must be renewed annually. Funeral directors attend conferences and workshops each year to stay current in their field.

Some people plan their funerals ahead of time, which can make things easier for their families.

Choosing a Community Service Career

Advancement Opportunities

Most directors start out on the staff of a funeral home. From there, they can work their way up to manage the funeral home. They may become a partner with a share in a home, or they may choose to buy and operate their own funeral home.

Job Growth and Salary Outlook

The U.S. Department of Labor forecasts a 12 percent increase in jobs in this field over the next ten years. There will be many new job openings in this field. In 2006, a funeral home director employed as staff made an average of $38,543. However, branch managers made more, for an average of $50,205. Those who owned their own funeral home made the most. The average salary of a funeral home director/owner was $75,737.[3] In 2006, 20 percent of funeral home directors were self-employed.[4]

How Can I Learn More?

Talk with a funeral home director in your area about your interest. Before you pursue a degree in mortuary science, get some experience to see if this is a good fit for you. Take a summer job at a funeral home. Learn what you can about your own family's funerary customs. Contact the National Funeral Directors Association. They offer information for people considering this career path.[5]

The best way to figure out if a career as a funeral director is right for you is to work in a funeral home. You can at least get an idea of what it takes to run one.

Choosing a Community Service Career

Surprising Fact

McFarlane was surprised to find that he did not have to wear a suit all the time. Part of owning your own funeral home is mowing the lawn and washing the cars.

Is This Career for You?

If you are interested in becoming a funeral director, think about the following questions:

- Would you enjoy arranging the details for an important ceremony?
- Do you feel good about yourself when you help someone who is going through a tough time?
- Would you be willing to wear formal clothes and keep a neat appearance?
- Are you thoughtful and kind?
- Would you like to run or own a business?
- Are you discreet and tactful?
- Would you be willing to learn how to prepare a body for burial or cremation?
- Are you flexible? Could you be ready and available whenever you might be needed?

Chapter 2. Police Officers

1. Bureau of Labor Statistics, U.S. Department of Labor, "Police and Detectives," *Occupational Outlook Handbook, 2010–11 Edition,* December 17, 2009, <http://www.bls.gov/oco/ocos160.htm> (April 7, 2011).

2. Ibid.

3. Ibid.

4. Ibid.

Chapter 3. EMTs

1. Bureau of Labor Statistics, U.S. Department of Labor, "Emergency Medical Technicians and Paramedics," *Occupational Outlook Handbook, 2010–11 Edition,* December 17, 2009, <http://www.bls.gov/oco/ocos101.htm> (April 7, 2011).

2. Ibid.

3. National Association of Emergency Medical Technicians, "EMS FAQ," *About EMS and Careers,* n.d., <http://www.naemt.org/aboutEMSAndCa-reers/ems_faq.htm> (April 29, 2008).

4. Bureau of Labor Statistics.

5. Ibid.

Chapter 4. Firefighters

1. Bureau of Labor Statistics, U.S. Department of Labor, "Fire Fighting Occupations," *Occupational Outlook Handbook, 2010–11 Edition*, December 17, 2009, <http://www.bls.gov/oco/ocos329.htm> (April 7, 2011).

2. Ibid.

3. Michael Farr, *100 Fastest-Growing Careers*, 11th ed. (Indianapolis, Ind.: JIST Works, 2010), p. 130.

4. Ronny J. Coleman, *Opportunities in Fire Protection Career Services* (Chicago: VGM Career Books, 2003), p. 91.

5. Bureau of Labor Statistics.

Chapter 5. Social Workers

1. Bureau of Labor Statistics, U.S. Department of Labor, "Social Workers," *Occupational Outlook Handbook, 2010–11 Edition*, December 17, 2009, <http://www.bls.gov/oco/ocos060.htm> (April 7, 2011).

2. Interview with Jennifer Stone, January 14, 2008.

3. Bureau of Labor Statistics.

4. Ibid.

Chapter 6. Teachers

1. "Summary Report for: Special Education Teachers, Preschool, Kindergarten, and Elementary School," *O*NET Online*, 2010, <http://www.onetonline.org/link/summary/25-2041.00> (April 7, 2011).

2. Michael Farr, *100 Fastest-Growing Careers*, 11th ed. (Indianapolis, Ind.: JIST Works, 2010), p. 281.

3. Bureau of Labor Statistics, U.S. Department of Labor, "Teachers—Kindergarten, Elementary, Middle, and Secondary," *Occupational Outlook Handbook, 2010–11 Edition*, December 17, 2009, <http://www.bls.gov/oco/ocos318.htm> (April 7, 2011).

4. Farr, p. 281.

Chapter 7. Clergypeople

1. "Summary Report for: Clergy," *O*NET Online*, 2010, <http://www.onetonline.org/link/summary/21-2011.00> (April 7, 2011).

2. Interview with Laura Holt-Haslam, January 26, 2008.

3. "Summary Report for: Clergy."

4. "Salary Snapshot for Minister Jobs," *PayScale*, March 31, 2011, <http://www.payscale.com/research/US/Job=Minister/Salary> (April 7, 2011).

5. Interview with John Haslam, April 28, 2008.

Chapter 8. Librarians

1. Bureau of Labor Statistics, U.S. Department of Labor, "Librarians," *Occupational Outlook Handbook, 2010–11 Edition*, December 17, 2009, <http://www.bls.gov/oco/ocos068.htm> (April 7, 2011).

2. "Library Workers: Facts and Figures," *Department for Professional Employees, AFL-CIO,* April 2010, <http://dpeaflcio.org/wp-content/uploads/2010/08/Library-workers-fact-sheet-2010.pdf> (April 7, 2011).

3. Interview with Melanie Taylor, February 9, 2008.

4. Bureau of Labor Statistics.

5. Ibid.

6. Interview with Melanie Taylor, February 9, 2008.

Chapter 9. Child-Care Workers

1. Bureau of Labor Statistics, U.S. Department of Labor, "Child Care Workers," *Bureau of Labor Statistics' Occupational Outlook Handbook, 2010–11 Edition,* December 17, 2009, <http://www.bls.gov/oco/ocos170.htm> (April 7, 2011).

2. Ibid.

3. Michael Farr, *100 Fastest-Growing Careers,* 11th ed. (Indianapolis, Ind.: JIST Works, 2010), p. 73.

4. Bureau of Labor Statistics.

Chapter 10. Postal Workers

1. Bureau of Labor Statistics, U.S. Department of Labor, "Postal Service Mail Carriers," *Occupational Outlook Handbook, 2010–11 Edition,* December 17, 2009, <http://www.bls.gov/oco/ocos141.htm> (April 7, 2011).

2. "Employee Testimonials," *U.S. Postal Service,* n.d., <http://www.usps.com/employment/_pdf/curr_testimonials1.pdf> (April 7, 2011).

3. Bureau of Labor Statistics.

4. "Postal Service Needs Help Preventing Dog Bites," *U.S. Postal Service,* May 13, 2010, <http://www.usps.com/communications/newsroom/2010/pr10_052.htm> (April 7, 2011).

Chapter 11. Funeral Directors

1. Bureau of Labor Statistics, U.S. Department of Labor, "Funeral Directors," *Bureau of Labor Statistics' Occupational Outlook Handbook, 2010–11 Edition*, December 17, 2009, <http://www.bls.gov/oco/ocos011.htm> (April 7, 2011).

2. Interview with Jeremy McFarlane, February 2008.

3. "NFDA Releases Results of Member Compensation Survey," *National Funeral Directors Association*, April 15, 2008, <http://www.nfda.org/news-a-events/all-press-releases/1216.html> (April 7, 2011).

4. U.S Department of Labor, *Occupational Outlook Handbook 2009* (New York: Skyhorse Publishing, Inc., 2008), p. 58.

5. "NFDA Provides Tool to Attract New Funeral Directors," *National Funeral Directors Association*, March 18, 2004, <http://nfda.org/news-a-events/all-press-releases/1265.html> (April 7, 2008).

accredited—Recognized as meeting certain standards.

apprentice—A person who learns a trade by working under the guidance of a skilled worker.

arson—The crime of setting fire to a building or other property.

baby boomer—A person who was born after World War II, during a peak in the birthrate in the United States.

bachelor's degree—A title earned when a person successfully completes a four-year program at a university or college.

certified—Having met the standards and recognized as official.

cremains—A term for the ashes remaining after cremation.

cremation—The burning of a dead body to reduce it to ashes.

dispatcher—A person who answers emergency calls and sends immediate help.

doctorate degree (PhD)— The highest college or university degree, requiring four or more years of study at the college level beyond a bachelor's degree.

game warden—A state police officer who specializes in fishing, boating, and hunting laws.

job shadowing—A program for high-school students to find out what it is like to be in a specific profession.

lay minister—A practicing minister who has not undergone the training to be ordained.

master's degree—An advanced degree requiring two years of additional college study after the completion of a bachelor's degree.

median—Average; the middle point in a series of numbers.

meticulous—Thorough and careful.

multitask—To do several tasks at one time.

obituary—A public notice of a person's death.

ordained—Given authority to be a minister by the church.

overtime—Hours beyond that of a normal work schedule.

pastor—A term for a minister; clergyperson.

patrol—To provide security to an area.

pension—A fixed amount of money paid to an employee after he or she retires.

probation—A trial period to determine whether a candidate is suitable for a job.

self-employed—Earning income from your own business, rather than as wages from an employer.

volunteer—To work for no pay.

Further Reading

Bolles, Richard Nelson. *What Color Is Your Parachute? 2008: A Practical Manual for Job-Hunters and Career Changers*. Berkeley, Calif.: Ten Speed Press, 2007.

Farr, Michael. *Best Jobs for the 21st Century*, fourth edition. Indianapolis, Ind.: JIST Works, 2006.

Llewellyn, A. Bronwyn, and Robin Holt. *The Everything Career Tests Book: Ten Tests to Determine the Right Occupation for You*. Cincinnati, Ohio: Adams Media Corporation, 2007.

Shontz, Priscilla K., and Richard A. Murray, eds. *A Day in the Life: Career Options in Library and Information Science*. Westport, Conn.: Libraries Unlimited, 2007.

Zichy, Shoya, and Ann Bidou. *Career Match: Connecting Who You Are With What You'll Love to Do*. New York: AMACOM, 2007.

Choosing a Community Service Career

Internet Addresses

Careers: Kids.gov
  <http://www.kids.gov/6_8/6_8_careers.shtml>

Exploring Career Information from the Bureau
  of Labor Statistics, 2010-2011 Edition:
  What Do You Like?
  <http://www.bls.gov/k12/>

U.S. Department of Labor Occupational
  Outlook Handbook 2010-2011 Edition
  <http://www.bls.gov/oco/home.htm>

further information,
21–22
job growth, 21
motivations, 13, 17
overview, 9, 11–16
salary, 13, 21
skills required, 13, 19
training, education,
17–19
postal workers
advancement, 103
benefits, drawbacks, 99
further information, 104
job growth, 103–104
motivations, 95, 99
overview, 12, 95–99,
105
salary, 95
skills required, 95, 101
training, education,
100–103
postmaster general, 103
public-service workers
generally, 7–12

R

rabbis. *see* clergypeople

S

social worker certification,
50–51
social workers
advancement, 51
benefits, drawbacks, 47
further information, 53
job growth, 52
motivations, 44, 49

overview, 11, 44–47,
53, 109
salary, 44, 52
skills required, 44, 50
training, education, 49
state troopers, 15
SWAT teams, 16

T

teachers
advancement, 63–64
benefits, drawbacks,
60–61
further information, 64
job growth, outlook, 64
motivations, 54, 58–60
overview, 11, 54–58, 65
salary, 54, 64
skills required, 54, 61
training, education, 63
teasing, 47

U

United States National Fire
Academy, 41

V

veterans, job preference for,
100, 104

W

wakes, 108
working overtime, 38